my
make it you.

your

Sew with Style | Easy Step-by-Step Instructions | Uniquely You

space

Shannon Mullen

C&T PUBLISHING

Text © 2007 Husqvarna Viking, Pfaff, and C&T Publishing, Inc.

Artwork © 2007 C&T Publishing, Inc.

Publisher: Amy Marson

Editorial Director: Gailen Runge

Acquisitions Editor: Jan Grigsby

Editor: Kesel Wilson

Technical Editors: Carolyn Aune and Teresa Stroin

Copyeditor/Proofreader: Wordfirm Inc.

Design Director/Book Designer: Kristy K. Zacharias

Illustrator: Tim Manibusan

Production Coordinator: Kirstie L. Pettersen

Photography by C&T Publishing, Inc., unless otherwise noted

Published by C&T Publishing, Inc., P.O. Box 1456, Lafayette, CA 94549

Library of Congress Cataloging-in-Publication Data

Mullen, Shannon Nina.

  Make it you--your space : sew with style--easy step-by-step instructions, uniquely you / Shannon Mullen.

     p. cm.

  ISBN-13: 978-1-57120-421-9 (paper trade : alk. paper)

  ISBN-10: 1-57120-421-0 (paper trade : alk. paper)

 1. House furnishings. 2. Household linens. 3. Machine sewing. I. Title.

  TT387.M95 2007

  746.9--dc22

           2006035400

Printed in China

10 9 8 7 6 5 4 3 2 1

Robert Marrott/RPM Images

HELLO!

What expresses your personal style as much as what you wear? The style of "your space." In this small corner of the big world you can display your passions, your attitude, and your creativity. You have the power to design with little money, little time, and little effort!

Whether you are in your first home, an apartment, or a dorm room or you just have a bedroom to decorate, your space is you! All the projects in this book will enhance these areas and can be made in different colors, embellished, or restyled to fit *you* perfectly.

I truly hope not only that you are successful with the projects you choose to make but also that you relax, enjoy, and grab hold of the creativity that is already yours. What are you waiting for?! Go ahead, make it you.

With love,

Shannon Mullen

And all of us at Husqvarna Viking, Pfaff, RJR Fabrics, C&T Publishing, and CK Media

*** table of contents

Supplies You'll Need

Like most hobbies, sewing requires some basic tools and supplies to make the experience satisfying. This chapter addresses the general supplies and equipment that you'll need to make the projects in this book. Refer to each project for the specific items needed.

✳ fabric 411

DEFINITIONS

* The finished tightly woven edges of fabric are called **selvages**. These should be cut off before using the fabric.

* Because fabric is woven, it has **grain lines**. Threads that travel parallel to the selvages are on the **lengthwise grain**, and threads that run perpendicular to the selvages are on the **crosswise grain**.

* Cutting or sewing on the **straight of grain** refers to cutting or sewing fabric along one of the grainlines.

* Cutting or sewing **on the bias** refers to cutting or sewing fabric diagonally across the grainlines (fabric stretches along the bias).

* Most fabric has a **right side** (the side that is printed) and a **wrong side** (the side that is not printed). Some fabrics, such as batiks and solids, look the same on both sides. For these fabrics, you don't have to worry about right or wrong sides.

GENERAL ADVICE

* Fabric is sold by the yard and you can purchase it in ⅛-yard increments. Before using a fabric, trim off the selvages.

FABRIC The projects in this book were all made from 100% cotton fabrics designed by **RJR Fabrics**. You can use whatever type of fabric you are comfortable working with and that provides the look you want. Be aware that different types of fabrics have different characteristics and may not provide the same look as the projects in the photographs. All the yardages given for the projects are based on fabric that is 42″ to 44″ wide.

selvages

bias

lengthwise grain

right side

wrong side

⟵ crosswise grain ⟶

Yardage and Inches

YARDAGE	INCHES	YARDAGE	INCHES
1/8 yard	4 1/2″	1 1/8 yards	40 1/2″
1/4 yard	9″	1 1/4 yards	45″
1/3 yard	12″	1 1/3 yards	48″
3/8 yard	13 1/2″	1 3/8 yards	49 1/2″
1/2 yard	18″	1 1/2 yards	54″
5/8 yard	22 1/2″	1 5/8 yards	58 1/2″
2/3 yard	24″	1 2/3 yards	60″
3/4 yard	27″	1 3/4 yards	63″
7/8 yard	31 1/2″	1 7/8 yards	67 1/2″
1 yard	36″	2 yards	72″

SEWING MACHINE A basic sewing machine with a straight stitch and zigzag capabilities is really all that is required. Of course, if your machine has decorative stitches, you can use them to add your own creative touch to the projects.

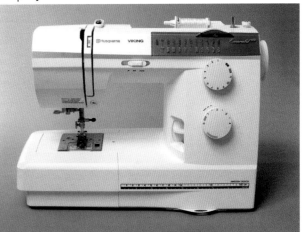

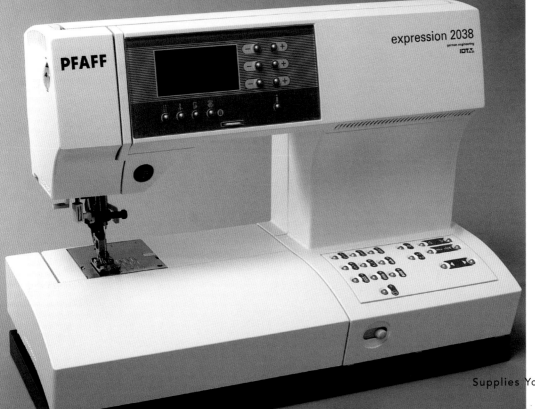

ROTARY CUTTING EQUIPMENT The rotary cutter has revolutionized the sewing world. It makes cutting fabric easier, faster, and more accurate. The tool looks like a pizza cutter, but the blade is retractable and can cut through several layers of fabric at once. I recommend a rotary cutter with a 45-mm or 60-mm blade for the projects in this book. Always rotary cut on a self-healing mat made especially for this task. The mat will protect your table surface and the cutter blade. An 18″ × 24″ mat is a good size to start with. Store your mat flat and away from direct sunlight when you are not using it.

You will also need a rotary cutting ruler to measure the fabric pieces and help you guide the cutter. These clear rulers are usually marked in ⅛″ increments. A 6″ × 24″ ruler is a good all-purpose size.

THREAD Good-quality thread is vital to the success of your project. Avoid purchasing bargain-bin threads. They tend to create a lot of lint, break often, and cause skipped stitches (where the bottom and top threads don't catch each other) and *lots* of frustration. Threads come in various weights and fibers. For the construction of most of the projects in this book, use a 50-weight all-purpose thread made from cotton, polyester, or a cotton-polyester blend. Top-stitching thread, which is heavier (thicker), is used to add decorative elements to several projects in this book. Many other threads, such as rayons and metallics, are also wonderful for embellishing.

PINS AND NEEDLES Make sure you have plenty of sharp pins on hand for holding pieces together. Throw away any pins that are bent or can't be easily inserted into the fabric.

The size and type of sewing machine needle you use will depend on the machine, the fabric, and the thread weight. The cotton fabrics used in this book were sewn with an 80/12 sharp or universal needle unless otherwise stated. Top-stitching was done with a top-stitch needle, which has a larger eye and thicker shaft to accommodate the thickness of top-stitching thread. Use a new sewing machine needle after eight hours of sewing time to prevent skipped stitches or pulling on the fabric threads. You will occasionally need a hand sewing needle. Purchase a package of sharps in assorted sizes and you'll be sure to have the one you need to accommodate most woven fabric weights.

You should press, not iron, your seams.

*** pressing 411**

DEFINITIONS

When you iron, you move the iron over the fabric in a back-and-forth or sweeping motion.

When you press, you move the iron with an up-and-down motion, holding the iron in place for a short period (three to five seconds).

When you press a seam allowance open, you open the seam up and press one seam allowance to each side of the seam. Sometimes, though, you'll be instructed to press a seam allowance to one side.

GENERAL ADVICE

You should press, not iron, your seams.

If the pressing direction is not indicated in the instructions, press your seam allowances toward the darker fabric so they won't show through.

Pressing a seam allowance to one side creates a stronger seam than pressing the seam allowance open, but pressing it open may reduce bulk. Seam allowances are often pressed open in garment sewing.

IRON AND IRONING SURFACE

Pressing is an important part of sewing. Keep an iron near your sewing area for this task. A portable pressing pad is a good alternative to a full-size ironing board if space is limited. Although you won't always use steam, an iron with this feature is recommended.

TAPE MEASURE Use a 60″ or 120″ long flexible synthetic or fiberglass tape measure for taking accurate measurements.

SHEARS AND SCISSORS Invest in a good pair of shears for cutting fabric pieces that can't be cut with a rotary cutter. Use these shears to cut fabric only. A smaller pair of scissors is also handy for clipping threads.

SEAM RIPPER I'm sure you'd rather not undo what you have sewn, but if your stitches look junky, bunchy, crooked, or are in the wrong place, just rip them out. You can "reverse sew" anything with a seam ripper. It is one of the most inexpensive and reliable sewing tools you will ever use!

INTERFACING You can apply interfacing to the wrong side of a fabric to give it support, add shape, reinforce an area, or prevent an area from stretching. Interfacing comes in a variety of weights, types, and textures and can be woven or non woven, fusible, or sew-in.

MARKING TOOLS Many devices can be used to mark fabric. My favorites are a water-soluble marker and a chalk wheel. Always be sure to test your marking tool on a scrap of the fabric you will be working with to make sure the marks can be seen and then removed.

EMBELLISHMENTS For a fun look, consider embellishments such as buttons, beads, crystals, glitter, decorative trim, and cording.

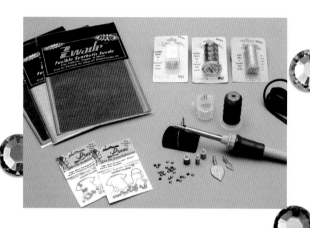

PROJECT GUIDE Watch for the following symbols that indicate the degree of difficulty (or ease) of each project. One symbol indicates the easiest project and three indicates the most challenging.

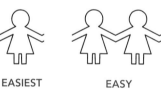

EASIEST   EASY   MORE CHALLENGING

Always test your marking tool on scrap fabric first!

bathro

Sink  skirt

Turn a wall-mounted sink into extra storage space while adding color and style to your bathroom or kitchen. This sink skirt is a great way to keep those extra items out of sight for a neat, uncluttered look!

Supplies

* 2½–3 yards fabric (see Cutting Step 2 for the exact amount you need)
* 1½–2 yards 1½"-wide hook-and-loop tape with a stick-on hook side and a sew-on loop side (see Cutting Step 1 for the exact amount you need)
* 90/14 needle
* Basic supplies

Cutting

1. Measure around 3 sides of your sink and cut a strip of hook-and-loop tape this length.

2. Measure from the place on the sink edge you want the top of the skirt to be to the floor and add 5¼" to obtain the sink skirt length. Cut a piece of fabric this wide by 2 times the measurement determined in Step 1.

NOTE: For the sink skirt shown, the lengthwise grain of the fabric runs horizontally in the skirt. If you have a directional print that runs up and down the fabric, you will need to cut 2 pieces the sink skirt length (determined above) by the width of the fabric and sew them together side to side. (see One-way Designs 411, page 38)

Instructions

Sew all pieces right sides together, using a ½" seam allowance.

1. Fold over each side of the sink skirt ½" and press. Fold over an additional 1" and press. Sew the side hems with a straight stitch close to the inside fold.

2. Fold over the bottom edge ½" and press. Fold over an additional 3" and press. Sew the bottom hem with a straight stitch close to the inside fold.

3. Select a medium-width zigzag stitch and stitch along the raw top edge of the skirt to prevent the fabric from unraveling. Fold over the top edge 2" and pin in place.

4. Machine baste close to this folded edge; if your machine does not have a preset basting stitch, use a straight stitch with a long stitch length (4.0). Sew another row of basting ¼″ below the first one. Sew 2 more rows of basting, one ⅜″ down from the second row and another ¼″ below that. Sew another 2 rows of basting, one ⅜″ down from the fourth row and another ¼″ below that. You will have 6 rows of basting stitches.

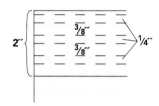

*** basting 411**

Machine basting involves using a straight stitch with a long stitch length (at least 4.0 mm) to temporarily hold two fabrics together. This type of seam is usually removed later and can also be used to gather or ease fabric. Using a contrasting thread color will make the removal of the stitches easier.

5. Separate the bobbin (bottom) thread from the top threads; hold the bobbin threads and gently slide the fabric along the threads. This will gather the top of the skirt. Continue to draw up the threads until the fabric is the width needed to wrap around the sink. Tie the thread tails at both ends to secure the gathers. Distribute the gathers evenly.

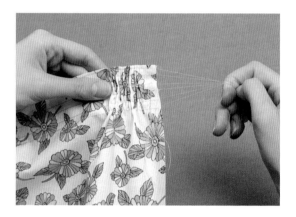

6. With a straight stitch of regular length (2.5), stitch down the center of each of the 3 pairs of gathered basting-stitch rows. Take care that the gathers remain evenly distributed. Completely remove the basting stitches.

7. With a straight stitch, stitch the loop half of the hook-and-loop tape to the back of the skirt, stitching through the tape and skirt right over the top and bottom rows of regular-length gathering stitches.

8. Peel off the backing from the hook half of the hook-and-loop tape and apply the tape to the sink edge. Attach the skirt and enjoy your new look!

Sew Fun!

If you enjoy embroidery, cut a band of solid fabric to the width of the sink skirt and finish all the edges. Embroider on it and stitch it to the bottom or top hem of the sink skirt for a beautiful addition of color and texture. You can also pleat the skirt instead of gathering it.

Sew You!

Piece together left over fabric, old jeans, shirts, or skirts for a retro-redo look!

valance

Company is coming and you need a quick pick-me-up for your room. This valance is the perfect fit. It's a quick project that will have your friends asking where you shop!

Supplies

The yardage given is for a 36″-wide window. Refer to Cutting to determine the yardage you need for your window.

* 1 yard base fabric
* 1¼ yards coordinating fabric
* Water-soluble marker
* Scallop ruler or template (optional; see the note on page 20)
* Edge-joining, or stitch in-the-ditch, foot (optional; see the note on page 21)
* Curtain rod
* Basic supplies

Cutting

1. Hang the curtain rod and measure it end-to-end.

2. Multiply the length of the rod by 2 to obtain the width for the gathered valance.

* curtain gathers 411

A gathered curtain or valance is generally 1½ to 2 times as wide as the curtain rod is long.

A straight valance (ungathered) is as wide as the curtain rod.

3. From the base fabric, cut 2 strips 14″ by the width of the fabric.

4. From the coordinating fabric, cut 2 strips 18″ by the width of the fabric.

NOTE: If you have a decorative curtain rod with a larger circumference, cut the piece of coordinating fabric larger to accommodate the rod. Measure the circumference of the rod and add at least 2″ to that. Add that total to 14″ to determine the size to cut the coordinating fabric.

Instructions

Sew all pieces right sides together, using a ½″ seam allowance.

1. Sew the base fabric strips together end-to-end to create one long strip and trim the unit to the width calculated in Cutting Step 2. Press the seam allowances open. Repeat with the coordinating fabric strips.

2. Match 1 long edge of the base and coordinating strips right sides together and sew. Press the seam allowance open. Align the other long raw edges right sides together and pin. The coordinating fabric will come over the front to create the casing for the curtain rod.

3. Fold the valance in half, matching the short sides. Starting at the fold at the center of the bottom raw edge, mark half a scallop with the scallop ruler or template and a water-soluble marker. Make sure the bottom of the scallop is at least ½″ from the bottom edge of the valance. Continue along the rest of the bottom raw edge, marking full scallops to the end. Unfold the valance, and mark in the same manner to the other end. You may end up with a partial scallop at each end, but that is okay.

NOTE: You can also use a 7″ or larger plate as a scallop template to draw an arc.

4. Sew along the marked line and then trim the seam allowance to ¼″. Make a straight cut into the point of each scallop, being careful not to cut the stitching. Trim the seam allowance in each point to about ⅛″ away from the stitching. Turn the valance right side out and press.

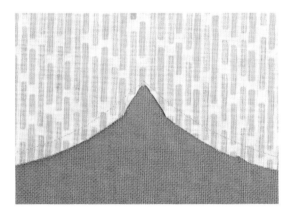

5. Using a zigzag stitch, finish the raw edge at the short ends of the valance. Fold the edge under ¼″, wrong sides together, to the inside and press. Topstitch close to the folded edge.

6. Smooth the fabric from the scalloped edge toward the top of the valance and press the top edge to create the casing.

7. With a straight stitch, sew in the seam where the coordinating and base fabrics meet to form the rod casing. This technique is called stitching in-the-ditch.

NOTE: An edge-joining, or stitch-in-the-ditch, foot makes this step easier because you can place the flange of the edge-joining foot right in the seam and stitch. Check with your local sewing machine dealer to see if one is available for your machine.

* * stitch in-the-ditch 411

Stitching in-the-ditch is a common sewing technique that involves sewing in the seam where two fabrics are joined. This technique is a great way of holding layers in place without visible stitches.

Sew You!

Before sewing the scalloped edges together, sew piping along the edge between the fabric layers to add an additional accent.

Sew Fun!

Getting tired of your valance? Flip it! This project is reversible and makes your valuable time better spent, as you are completing two projects instead of one!

Embellished towels

Personalizing towels with your sewing machine is the perfect way to learn creative sewing techniques while making wonderful accessories for your home and gifts for your friends.

Supplies

* Towels

* ¼ yard fabric for towel with pleated edge

* 1 yard ½˝– to ⅜˝–wide ribbon or decorative trim for towel with pleated edge

* Small pieces of coordinating fabrics for appliquéd towel

* Temporary fabric adhesive spray for appliquéd towel (optional)

* Make It You embroidery collection #2 from Cactus Punch for embroidered towel (optional)

* Aqua Magic water-soluble stabilizer for embroidered towel

* Melt-away stabilizer for embroidered towel

* 90/14 top-stitch needle

* Free-motion foot for appliquéd and embroidered towel

* Basic supplies

Instructions

Sew all pieces right sides together, using a ¼˝ seam allowance.

TOWELS WITH PLEATED FABRIC EDGING

1. Cut 2 strips 2½˝ by the width of the fabric.

2. Sew the strips together end-to-end to create one long strip. Cut the strip to a length 2 times the width of the towel. Finish the left end and the bottom long edge of the strip with a rolled edge, using either a sewing machine or a serger, or fold under the raw edge ¼˝, fold it again, and stitch close to the inside fold to make a hem.

3. Starting from the left, mark every 1½˝ along the long raw edge. Fold the strip so that the first mark meets the second. Finger-press the fold and pin in place.

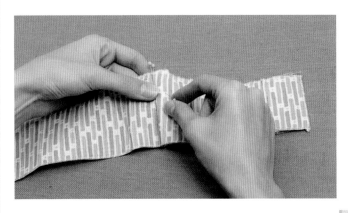

4. To form the next pleat, fold the strip so that the third mark meets the fourth. Press and pin. Continue folding at the marks to create pleats across the entire strip. Press the pleats in place and secure them by stitching ¼" from the top edge of the strip. Measure and trim the strip at the right end to the width of the towel and finish the end as described in Step 2.

5. Pin the stitched edge of the strip under the bottom edge of the towel, so the top of the fabric strip is covered by the hem of the towel. With a medium zigzag stitch (length 3.5, width 3.5), sew the edge of the pleated strip to the towel.

6. On the front side of the towel, place ribbon or decorative trim over the zigzag stitching, folding under the ends even with the towel edges, and topstitch in place with a straight stitch.

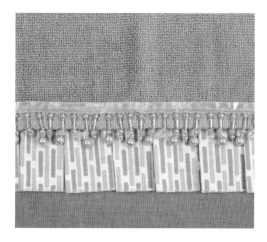

TOWELS WITH RAW-EDGE APPLIQUÉ

1. Cut around printed designs in fabric for appliqué shapes. Arrange them on the towel to create a pleasing design. Pin them securely in place or use temporary fabric adhesive spray to secure them to the towel.

2. Attach a free-motion foot to your sewing machine and lower the feed dogs.

3. Free-motion stitch around the appliqué shapes ¼" in from the outside edges. The raw edges will fray to create a funky look. You can also stitch within the printed designs of the fabric to create texture.

free-motion stitching 411

Free-motion stitching is done with the feed dogs lowered. You control the speed and direction of the fabric while sewing. This technique allows you to sew around odd shapes and create interesting designs with your stitching.

TOWELS WITH MACHINE EMBROIDERY

For this project, you will need a computerized sewing machine with an embroidery attachment.

1. Consult your sewing machine manual for machine embroidery instructions. Select a design and send it to the sewing machine.

2. Hoop the Aqua Magic stabilizer so the paper side is facing up. Use a straight pin to score through the paper layer only and peel it away to reveal the sticky layer. Place the towel on top of the stabilizer and press with your fingers to adhere it to the stabilizer.

3. Place a piece of melt-away stabilizer on top of the towel to keep the embroidery from sinking into the towel fibers. Baste in the hoop to hold all 3 layers together (Aqua Magic stabilizer, towel, melt-away stabilizer).

4. Embroider your design on the towel. Remove the basting stitches and tear off the excess stabilizer from the top and bottom. Using a medium setting on the iron, make small circular motions on top of the remaining melt-away stabilizer to make it disappear!

melt-away stabilizer **411**

Melt-away stabilizer helps you embroider on high-loft fabrics like towels and fleece without losing the stitching in the fabric.

Sew Fun!

For a really fun look, use a zigzag stitch to sew narrow ribbon in various designs or create vines and stems for the appliqué flowers. Or add some fun gemstones to the appliqués for a little glitz.

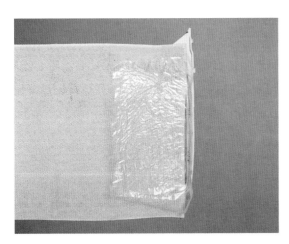

bedro

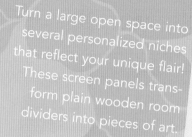

Turn a large open space into several personalized niches that reflect your unique flair! These screen panels transform plain wooden room dividers into pieces of art.

Screen panels

Supplies

The yardage given is for 3 screen panels, each 16″ × 40″. Measure the length and width of your panels to determine the yardage you need.

* ⅝ yard each of 5 coordinating fabrics
* 1¾ yards backing fabric
* Low-loft cotton batting at least 42″ × 56″
* 12 buttons approximately ⅝″ in diameter
* Decorative trim such as lace, braid, roping, or pearls (optional)
* Water-soluble marker
* 3-panel room divider
* Fasturn tool (optional)
* Basic supplies

Cutting

1. Measure the height and width of the panel you wish to cover and add 1″ to each measurement for seam allowances. These are the base dimensions.

2. From the backing fabric, cut 3 pieces the size of the base dimensions determined in Step 1.

3. From the 5 coordinating fabrics, cut various strips 2½″, 3½″, 4½″, and 5″ by the width of the fabric.

NOTE: The number of strips will depend on the size of your panel.

4. From the backing fabric, cut 3 strips 2″ by the width of the fabric for the buttoned ties.

Instructions

Sew all pieces right sides together, using a ½″ seam allowance, unless otherwise indicated.

1. Using a ¼″ seam allowance, piece the assorted coordinating fabric strips together until you have a panel that is at least the width of the base dimensions. Press the seam allowances toward the darker fabrics as you piece. Make 3 panels and trim them to the base dimensions.

2. Layer each panel as follows and sew around the edges, leaving a 4″–5″ opening at the center of the bottom edge:

BATTING + BACKING FABRIC RIGHT SIDE UP + PIECED PANEL WRONG SIDE UP

Remember to back tack at both ends of your opening (see Back Tacking 411, page 50).

3. Trim the seam allowances at the corners and turn the units right side out (see Trimming Corners 411, page 46). Hand sew the opening closed and press. Add decorative trim if desired.

4. Fold each 2″-wide backing strip in half, right sides together, and using a ¼″ seam allowance stitch along the long edges. Turn the tubes right side out and cut them into 9″ sections until you have 12 tubes total.

NOTE: Using a Fasturn tool makes turning fabric tubes quick and easy.

5. Fold the raw ends to the inside of the tubes, press, and topstitch close to each folded end. After consulting your sewing machine manual for instructions on making buttonholes, stitch a buttonhole the size of your decorative buttons about ⅝″ in from one end of each tube.

6. Sew a button to each tube at the end opposite the buttonhole. If you are using flat buttons, sew on the buttons loosely, leaving ¼″ of threads between the button and the fabric. After sewing on the button, wrap the thread several times around the ¼″ of threads between the button and fabric, insert the needle into the fabric, pull the thread through to the back, and then tie a knot. This "shank" will allow you to button through multiple layers without creating ripples.

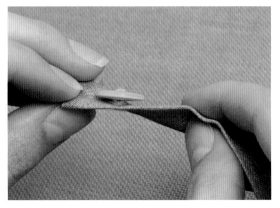

7. Button the tubes around each screen post. Place the screen flat on the floor with the panels on top and mark where each buttonhole needs to be on each panel to correspond to the tube button. Refer to your sewing machine manual to see how to sew buttonholes on the top and bottom of each panel. Button the panels to the tubes, wrapping the tube around the post.

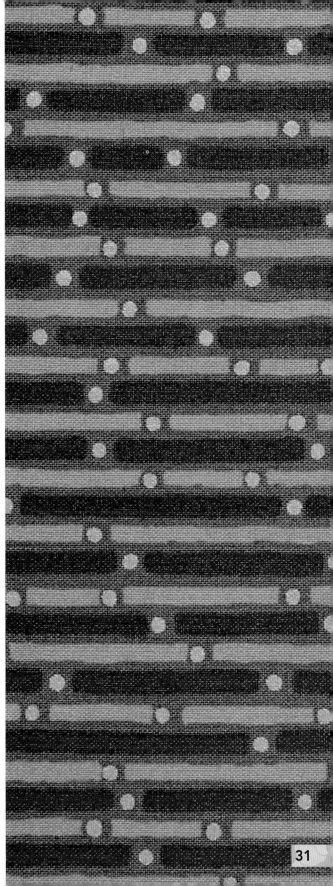

Framed fabrics

Create beautiful, one-of-a-kind pictures. Embellish fabric with thread using the free-motion thread-painting technique and add a creative touch by applying crystals or even paint to your canvas!

Supplies

* ½ yard large-print fabric

* 8″ × 10″ or 11″ × 17″ frame and mat

* 90/14 top-stitch needle

* Rayon decorative thread to match fabric motifs

* Tear-away stabilizer

* Water-soluble marker

* Gluestick

* Free-motion embroidery foot

* 1″-wide coordinating grosgrain ribbon (optional)

* Tsukineko fabric inks (optional)

* Kandi Corp hot-fix decorative applicator to apply heat-activated crystals (optional)

* Heat-activated crystals (optional)

* Basic supplies

Instructions

1. Remove the mat from the frame and place the mat on the large-print fabric so that it frames the design elements you want to feature. Mark around the framed image with a water-soluble marker and cut the fabric 2″ outside the marked line. Framing and cutting a piece of fabric with the exact design elements you want is called *fussy cutting*.

2. Thread your machine with a rayon decorative thread. Drop the feed dogs and select a straight stitch. Place tear-away stabilizer under the fabric to prevent it from puckering while you sew. Lower the presser foot before sewing to engage the tension on the top thread.

3. Use your hands to guide the fabric in a side-to-side or up-and-down motion under the needle. This technique is called *thread painting*. If you have a speed-control setting on your machine, find a comfortable speed that helps you get a consistent stitch length.

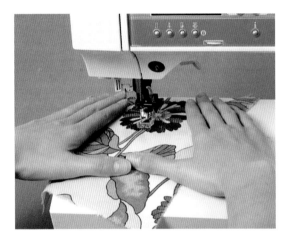

✱ *thread painting* 411

Free-motion fabric embellishment uses a straight stitch with the feed dogs lowered. The fabric can be placed in a hoop, or you can sew with a free-motion foot or a darning foot. Consult your sewing machine manual for free-motion and darning settings.

4. For additional embellishment, use Kandi Corp's hot-fix decorative applicator to apply crystals and pearls or use Tsukineko inks to paint original designs. Make sure you allow the ink to dry before you frame the fabric.

5. Center the mat over your thread-painted fabric and turn them both over so that the back of the fabric is facing you. Use a glue-stick to tack the edges of the fabric to the mat. Turn the mat right side up. Using a straight stitch (length 3.5) and the 90/14 top-stitch needle, sew the fabric to the mat by stitching ½″ from the inside edge of the mat. For a fun touch, you can glue or sew grosgrain ribbon around the mat. Add the frame and hang your masterpiece!

Sew You!

Why not try a complete room makeover? Stretch your fabric over a large canvas and make it into a one-of-a-kind headboard! See a cool example at www.makeitu.com.

Sew Fun!

Mount your thread-painted fabric on an artist's canvas with a staple gun. These canvases are available in all arts and crafts stores. Simply pull the fabric over the edges of the canvas and secure the fabric in place with a staple every three or four inches.

Fabric Wallpaper border

Fabric is the perfect alternative to paper wallpaper. Because you can remove fabric easily without damaging your walls, you can change your décor anytime you choose. Make it you!

Supplies

* Light- to medium-weight fabric (see Instructions Steps 1 and 2 for determining yardage)

* Ribbon to finish the edges of the fabric border (optional)

* Liquid fabric starch (available in grocery stores)

* Clean sponge, paintbrush, or paint roller

* Basic supplies

Instructions

1. Determine the length of the walls you want to add borders to. Determine the width of the border, being sure to pick a width that complements the designs within the fabric. A standard ceiling border is 6″–9″ wide.

2. Look at the print in the fabric to see how many times the design is repeated across the fabric width. In large-print fabrics, the design is often repeated twice across so that you will be able to cut 2 matching borders from the width of the fabric. With smaller prints you may be able to get up to 5 border strips from the width of the fabric. Sometimes the repeated designs are offset across the width of the fabric, but you can still cut matching lengthwise strips from them. To determine your yardage requirements, divide the total length of the walls you need to cover by the number of border strips you can cut from the width of the fabric. Add at least 1½ yards to ensure the proper matching of prints.

3. Lay out the fabric on the cutting mat. Paying attention to the printed design, cut one strip the full length of the fabric by the predetermined width. Before the next cut, line up the end of the first strip with the uncut fabric until the designs match. This step will tell you where the second strip cut should start. Repeat this process until you have cut enough strips for the entire border.

one-way designs 411

Fabrics with one-way designs, also called directional fabrics, are fabrics with designs running in one direction. These fabrics must always be cut in the same direction so that the designs will not be upside down or going in different directions on the finished project.

4. Place the finished strips together end-to-end on a flat surface and match the designs. You do not need seam allowances on the ends because the strips will be butted edge-to-edge on the wall.

5. Wash the wall area to remove any dirt. Apply starch to the wall where the first border strip will be placed. Smooth the fabric onto the wall with your hands and use pushpins to hold it in place temporarily.

6. Apply a thin coat of starch to the fabric surface, brushing and smoothing the fabric to remove bubbles and wrinkles. Be sure the starch penetrates the fabric evenly. Work your way around the room, putting up one border strip at a time. Use a clean sponge to remove excess starch from the wall. If you want to finish the top and bottom edges of the border with ribbon, apply the ribbon with starch in the same way as you did the fabric.

7. Change your mind? To remove the fabric border, simply peel the fabric off the wall. If it doesn't peel easily, use a sponge to dampen the fabric with water.

Sew You!

Why not put borders around your windows and doors too? Make the borders extra wide, so that an inch of the fabric overlaps onto the trim, then cut away the excess with a craft knife for a nice, tight fit.

Sew Fun!

Cut out large flowers or other motifs from a fabric design and paste them to your walls. Or if you're crazy for color, use this technique to cover your entire wall with fabric!

Fabric-Covered frames

Add contrast and accent to your décor by beautifully displaying photos of family and friends in fabric-covered picture frames. Why settle for plain when you can create something fabulous?

Supplies

The yardage given is for a 12″ × 12″ frame with a 5″ × 7″ photo insert. You may need different amounts of fabric depending on the size of your frame.

* ¼ yard dark fabric

* ¼ yard medium fabric

* ⅓ yard light fabric

* 1 package or ½ yard fusible fleece

* ⅜ yard paper-backed fusible web

* ¼″- or ½″-wide paper-backed fusible web tape

* Temporary fabric adhesive spray

* 12″ × 12″ picture frame with wide borders

* Decorative threads, buttons, lace, trims, or beads (optional)

* Tear-away stabilizer (if doing decorative stitching)

* Basic supplies

Cutting

1. From the dark fabric, cut 1 rectangle 7¼″ × 6¼″.

2. From the medium fabric, cut 1 rectangle 7¼″ × 9¼″.

3. From the light fabric, cut 1 rectangle 8¼″ × 15″.

4. From the fusible fleece, cut 1 square 14″ × 14″.

Instructions

Sew all pieces right sides together, using a ¼″ seam allowance.

1. Sew the dark and medium fabric rectangles together along the 7¼″ edges and press the seam allowance toward the dark fabric. Sew the light fabric to the pieced unit along one long edge and press the seam allowance toward the pieced unit. You will end up with a 15″ × 15″ finished square of pieced fabric.

2. Following the manufacturer's instructions, fuse the fleece to the wrong side of the pieced square. If you would like to embellish the fabric in any way, do so now.

3. Remove the backing insert, glass, and hardware from the frame. Place strips of fusible tape along the back edges of the frame.

4. Apply the temporary fabric adhesive spray to the fleece square and press the square onto the front of the frame. Leave a consistent amount of overlap on all 4 edges.

5. Gently wrap the fabric over the sides of the frame and around to the back. Following the manufacturer's instructions, fuse the fabric in place.

6. In the picture frame opening, carefully cut an X from corner to corner in the fabric and fleece. Loosen the fleece from the fabric within the X and trim away the fleece to reduce the bulk. Pull the fabric through the opening and wrap it around to the back. Use fusible tape to fuse the fabric edges to the back of the frame.

7. To create a nice finished backing for the frame, cut an 11¾˝ × 11¾˝ square of fabric and fuse the fusible web to the wrong side of the fabric. Place the fused fabric right side up onto the back of the picture frame and fuse in place. Cut the picture area from the backing so that you have an opening in the frame.

8. Reattach all the hardware and insert the picture.

Sew Fun!

Change the ratio of the sizes of the fabric rectangles or change the number of fabrics you are using. Remember: working with odd numbers is more pleasing to the eye.

Sew You!

Embellish the pieced fabric with random lines of decorative stitches before you fuse it to the frame.

43

curtains

Curtains can make or break a room. Turn drab into delightful by designing them yourself. Make your room gorgeous inside and out!

Supplies

The yardage given is for 2 lined 40˝-wide × 81˝-long curtains. Measure the length and width of your window to determine the yardage you need. Fabric for gathered curtains is generally cut to 1½–2 times the width of the window.

* 4¼ yards patterned fabric for curtain

* 4¼ yards patterned fabric for lining

* 2½ yards solid fabric for bottom panel

* 1¼ yards medium or heavy fusible interfacing

* 4 yards 1˝-wide grosgrain ribbon

* 6 to 10 grommets ⁷⁄₁₆˝ size

* Grommet-setting tools

* ¼˝-wide paper-backed fusible web tape (optional)

* Curtain rod

* Basic supplies

Cutting

1. From both the curtain and lining fabrics, cut 2 pieces each 72˝ long by the width of the fabric.

2. From the bottom-panel fabric, cut 1 piece 2½ yards by the width of the fabric. Cut this piece in half lengthwise.

3. Cut the interfacing into 3˝-wide strips.

Instructions

Sew all pieces right sides together, using a ½˝ seam allowance.

1. On the wrong side of the curtain fabric, mark a line across the width of the fabric 7½˝ down from the top. Following the manufacturer's instructions, fuse 3˝ strips of interfacing end-to-end with the top edges of the strips along the marked line. The interfacing will add stability for the grommets.

7½˝

2. Sew one long side of the curtain fabric to one long side of the lining fabric. Press the seam allowance toward the darker fabric. Measure the width of the opened curtain/lining unit and cut the length of the bottom panel to match the width. Pin the bottom panel in place and sew. Press the seam allowance toward the curtain/lining unit.

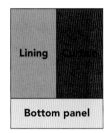

Lining | Curtain

Bottom panel

3. Fold the unit right sides together at the side seam, pin the raw edges together, and sew the remaining 3 edges of the curtain together, leaving a 4″–5″ opening along the bottom edge. Trim the corners and turn the curtain right side out. Press all the edges well. Turn in the seam allowances of the opening and hand sew it closed, or use ¼″ fusible tape to fuse it shut.

trimming corners 411

You trim a corner to reduce bulk. To clip a corner, cut off the corner of the sewn angle outside your stitching line, removing extra seam allowance.

Trim.

4. Fold the top of the curtain down 10″ to the front of the curtain so that the lining shows. This fold will create a faux valance.

5. Place a grommet 2″ below the folded top edge in the center of the faux valance and 1″ away from each side edge. You may choose to add additional grommets for greater support.

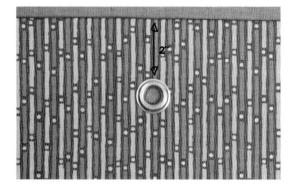

2″

6. Cut the grosgrain ribbon in 24″-long pieces and thread them through the grommets. Tie the curtain to the curtain rod. The best thing about these curtains is that you now have 2 sets! Simply turn the curtain to the "wrong side" so the lining is facing out and you have a completely different, yet coordinated look!

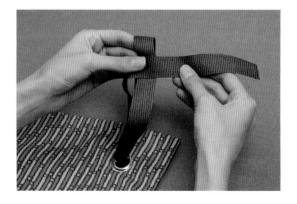

Sew You!

Cut an assortment of fabrics into squares and rectangles and piece them together for the curtain panel. The variety of colors can help you pull together a room or give you themed looks from bohemian to shabby chic.

Sew Fun!

Use this same technique to make a colorful shower curtain for your bathroom and see page 15 for how to make a matching sink skirt.

Bed canopy

This canopy turns your bed into a warm and cozy niche so you can sleep like royalty. Change the fabrics to fit your own personality and style.

Supplies

The sheer canopy used as the canopy base for this project can be purchased in the bed and bath section of a department store.

* Approximately 5 yards fabric for canopy (see Cutting Step 1)
* Approximately 5 yards contrasting fabric for lining (see Cutting Step 1)
* 3 yards ¾″-wide grosgrain ribbon
* Sheer canopy on a circular base
* 5 yards decorative ribbon (optional)
* Water-soluble marker
* Basic supplies

Cutting

1. Measure from the floor to the area that the canopy will be suspended from (usually about 7′) and add 4″. This measurement will be the canopy length.

2. From both the canopy and lining fabrics, cut 2 panels each to the above-measured length × the width of the fabric.

3. Cut the grosgrain ribbon in half so you have two 54″ pieces.

Instructions

Sew all pieces right sides together, using a ½″ seam allowance.

1. On the right side of 1 lining panel, use a water-soluble marker to mark a line across the width of the fabric 4″ from the top. Mark a second line 1″ down from this line. The area between the 2 lines will be the canopy casing. Repeat on the other lining panel.

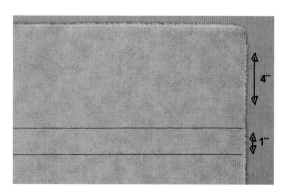

2. Sew 1 lining panel to 1 canopy panel, right sides together, around all 4 sides, leaving 5″ open along the bottom edge; do not sew in the 1″ casing area between the marked lines. Back tack when starting and stopping at each of these openings so the stitches are secure. Trim the corners, turn the panel right side out, and press the seams well. Avoid ironing over the marked lines because heat permanently sets water-soluble marks and you will not be able to remove them. Repeat with the second lining panel and canopy panel.

*back tacking 411

To back tack at the beginning and end of a seam, touch the reverse button on your sewing machine. This will prevent the stitches from unraveling.

3. Sew along the marked lines with a straight stitch to create the casings. Remove the water-soluble marked lines by spritzing water on them.

4. *Optional:* Cut the decorative ribbon in half and attach it just below the casing of each panel. Sew the ends of the ribbon at the edges of the panels and tack it down in the middle of each panel.

5. Thread the grosgrain ribbon through the casings of both panels and tie around the canopy base.

Sew You!

Knit together strips of fabric to create one-of-a-kind pull-back ties. You can also add a little sparkle to your canopy by securing crystals and glass beads to it.

Sew Fun!

If you want a super quick way to complete long seams, use a serger! These nifty machines are compact and do multiple steps at once. They cut, seam, and finish the edge all in one step, and they can also sew much faster than a sewing machine!

pillows

Cover your bed with personalized pillows! Once you have the basics of pillow making, you can mix and match any fabrics to get exactly the look you want.

Supplies

FOLDED GRID PILLOW

* ⅝ yard green fabric

* ½ yard fabric for pillow back

* Off-white #5 perle cotton thread

* Hand sewing needle with large eye

* 4 round mirrors 1″ in diameter

* 12 round mirrors ¾″ in diameter

* Fabric glue

* 16″ square pillow form

* Basic supplies

RIBBON BORDER PILLOW

* ¼ yard print fabric for pillow center

* ¼ yard dark pink print for borders

* ½ yard fabric for pillow back

* 2 yards green ribbon

* 16″ square pillow form

* Basic supplies

Folded Grid Pillow Cutting

1. From the green fabric, cut 1 square 18″ × 18″.

2. From the pillow back fabric, cut 2 rectangles 11″ × 15½″.

Folded Grid Pillow Instructions

Sew all pieces right sides together, using a ¼″ seam allowance.

1. Fold the green square in half and press to form a crease. Open the square and mark 3″ increments at the edge of the square (in the seam allowance) on each side of the pressed fold and press horizontal folds at the marks.

mark and fold	3″
mark and fold	3″
fold	3″
mark and fold	3″
mark and fold	3″
	3″

*pillow basics 411

Make the pillow fronts 1″ smaller than the pillow form so the pillows will be stuffed firmly. You can use polyester fiberfill instead of a pillow form if desired.

2. Stitch ¼″ from each fold and press the pleats all in one direction.

3. Repeat Steps 1 and 2, this time folding the square in half in the other direction. This process will give you a 6 × 6 grid.

4. Glue a mirror to the center of each square in the center 4 × 4 grid with a dab of fabric glue. Place the 1″ mirrors in the corner squares. Thread a hand sewing needle with 12″ of off-white perle cotton thread and

stitch the mirrors in place following the number order in the diagram. Tie off the threads on the wrong side of the pillow front.

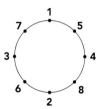

5. See Finishing Pillows (page 55).

Sew You!

For cute small pillows, make a 2 × 2 folded grid embellished with buttons and bordered by a different color fabric.

Sew Fun!

Pillows don't have to be square! Make rectangular pillows and add simple creative touches like piping between different colored fabrics.

Ribbon Border Pillow Cutting

1. From the print fabric, cut 1 square 7½″ × 7½″.

2. From the dark pink print, cut 2 strips 4½″ × 7½″ and 2 strips 4½″ × 15½″.

3. From the pillow back fabric, cut 2 rectangles 11″ × 15½″.

Ribbon Border Pillow Instructions

Sew all pieces right sides together, using a ¼″ seam allowance.

1. Sew one short dark pink strip to the print square along the 7½″ edge of the strip. Repeat to sew the other short strip to the opposite side of the square. Press the seam allowances toward the dark pink strips.

2. Place one long dark pink strip on each of the remaining sides of the print square. Stitch and press the seam allowances toward the dark pink strips.

3. Cut the ribbon into 4 equal lengths. Pin a ribbon strip to opposite sides of the center square and stitch along the long edge of each ribbon (refer to the photo on page 52). Repeat to stitch the other 2 ribbon strips to the remaining sides of the square. Trim off any excess ribbon.

4. See Finishing Pillows (below).

Finishing Pillows

1. Fold ¼″ over along one long edge of each pillow back rectangle and press. Fold over another ¼″ and press again. Stitch close to the first fold to secure the hem.

2. Place the pillow front right side up on a flat surface. With right sides together, place one of the pillow back pieces on the left and one on the right so that the raw edges of the front and back pieces meet. Match the raw edges and pin in place. The hemmed edges of the back pieces will overlap in the center. Sew around the outside edges only.

3. Trim the seam allowance at the corners to reduce bulk (see Trimming Corners 411, page 46). This trimming helps form a nice corner point when you turn the pillow cover right side out.

4. Turn the pillow cover right side out.

5. Place the pillow form or stuffing inside the pillow cover. Hand sew the opening closed.

quilt

What could be cozier than curling up under your own quilt? Brighten up your entire room by adding this unique piece to your collection and make pillows to match. The size of the finished quilt will be a cozy 45″ × 51″.

Supplies

* 1 yard large-print fabric
* ¾ yard small-print fabric
* ⅜ yard light pink fabric
* 1¼ yards dark pink fabric
* ⅜ yard green fabric
* 2⅞ yards fabric for backing
* 51″ × 57″ batting
* Basic supplies

Cutting

1. FROM THE LARGE-PRINT FABRIC:

Cut 3 strips 2½″ by the width of the fabric.

Cut 2 squares 12½″ × 12½″ from different areas of the fabric.

Cut 1 vertical rectangle 6½″ × 12½″.

Cut 4 squares 6½″ × 6½″ from different areas of the fabric.

2. FROM THE SMALL-PRINT FABRIC:

Cut 3 strips 2½″ by the width of the fabric.

Cut 1 horizontal rectangle 12½″ × 6½″.

Cut 4 squares 6½″ × 6½″ from different areas of the fabric.

3. FROM THE LIGHT PINK FABRIC:

Cut 3 strips 2½″ by the width of the fabric.

4. FROM THE DARK PINK FABRIC:

Cut 3 strips 2½″ by the width of the fabric.

Cut 2 strips 3½″ × 36½″.

Cut 2 strips 3½″ × 42½″.

Cut 4 squares 3½″ × 3½″.

Cut 5 strips 2¼″ by the width of the fabric.

5. FROM THE GREEN FABRIC:

Cut 2 strips 1¾″ × 36½″.

Cut 2 strips 1¾″ × 42½″.

Cut 4 rectangles 1¾″ × 3½″.

Cut 4 rectangles 1¾″ × 4¾″.

Instructions

Sew all pieces right sides together, using a ¼″ seam allowance.

"DANCING" NINE PATCH BLOCKS

1. Strip set A: Sew 1 strip of small-print fabric between 2 strips of dark pink fabric. Press the seam allowances toward the dark fabric. Trim the ends and cut the strip set into 16 units each 2½″ wide.

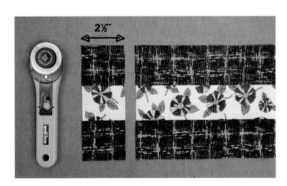

Strip set A

2. Strip set B: Sew 1 strip of dark pink fabric between 2 strips of small-print fabric. Press the seam allowances toward the dark fabric. Trim the ends and cut the strip set into 17 units each 2½″ wide. If you are not able to cut 17 units, you will need to make one more strip set.

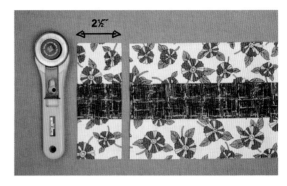

Strip set B

3. Nine-Patch blocks are made up of 3 rows of 3 squares. Sew the units together to make 5 Nine-Patch blocks with dark pink in the middle. Then make 6 with the small print in the middle.

Make 5.   Make 6.

"MOOSHY" NINE PATCH BLOCKS

1. Strip Set A: Sew 1 strip of light pink fabric between 2 strips of large-print fabric. Press the seam allowances toward the light fabric. Trim the ends and cut the strip set into 16 units each 2½″ wide.

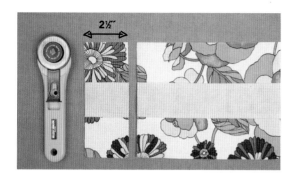

Strip set A

2. Strip Set B: Sew 1 strip of large-print fabric between 2 strips of light pink fabric. Press the seam allowances toward the light fabric. Trim the ends and cut the strip set into 17 units each 2½˝ wide. If you are not able to cut 17 units, you will need to make one more strip set.

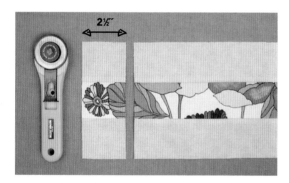

Strip set B

Sew You!

Use any of the block designs in the quilt to make matching pillows. Add tassels at the corners for a sophisticated look and embellish with hand-embroidered lines or designs!

3. Construct the Nine-Patch blocks as for the "Dancing" blocks. Make 5 Nine-Patch blocks with the large-print fabric in the middle. Then make 6 of the reverse.

Make 5. Make 6.

4. Refer to the quilt assembly diagram below to arrange the blocks. Stitch the blocks together in sections as shown, sew the sections into rows, and sew the rows together.

Finishing

These finishing instructions are simplified and assume that you have some knowledge of quiltmaking. If you are a beginner, consult one of the many wonderful books on quilt-making that deal with this subject in depth.

1. Sew a 36½″ green strip to each 36½″ dark pink outer border strip. Press the seam allowances toward the outer border. Sew a 42½″ green strip to each 42½″ dark pink outer border strip. Press the seam allowances toward the outer border. Sew the longer border strip units to the sides of the quilt.

2. To make a corner square, sew a 1¾″ × 3½″ green strip to one side of each 3½″ dark pink square of the outer border fabric. Then sew a 1¾″ × 4¾″ green strip to an adjacent side of each dark pink square. Press the seam allowances toward the square. Make 4 corner squares.

Make 4.

3. Sew a corner square to each end of the two 36½″ border units and sew the borders to the top and bottom of the quilt.

4. Layer the backing, batting, and quilt top. Pin baste.

5. Machine quilt in a diagonal grid to hold the layers together.

6. Bind the edges with the 2¼″ dark pink strips.

Check out 9-Patch Pizzazz by Judy Sisneros from C&T Publishing for more on making fun nine-patch quilts.

Covered Storage trunk

This is a great technique for anything that needs a facelift or for a piece of furniture such as an ottoman that you want to coordinate with your existing décor.

Supplies

The yardage is given for a trunk that measures 15˝ × 15˝ × 15˝. Measure your trunk to determine the yardage you need.

* 2 yards fabric for trunk
* ½ yard contrasting fabric for cording trim
* 2 yards ⅜˝ or ½˝ home décor piping cord
* 2 packages ¾˝-wide double-fold bias binding
* 1 roll ¼˝- or ½˝-wide paper-backed fusible tape (optional)
* Craft glue or hot glue gun
* 1 yard batting and temporary fabric adhesive spray (if your trunk does not already have a padded surface)
* Trunk
* Basic supplies

Cutting

1. Measure the length and width of the trunk lid (including the height of the sides) and add 2˝ to each of these dimensions.

2. Measure completely around the base of the trunk and add 1˝. Measure the height of the trunk and add 3˝. These are the base dimensions.

3. From the trunk fabric, cut a piece equal in size to the lid dimensions and a piece equal to the base dimensions.

4. From the contrasting fabric, cut enough 2½˝-wide bias strips to total the measurement around the lid plus 15˝.

Instructions

Sew all pieces right sides together, using a ½˝ seam allowance.

1. Remove all the hardware from the trunk. Turn the lid upside down and apply fusible tape along the inside lip. If you use glue, there is no need for the fusible tape.

2. If your trunk isn't padded, cut pieces of batting equal to the lid measurements, apply adhesive spray to one side of the batting, attach the fabric to the batting. Spray the other side of the batting and attach it to the lid. Place the trunk lid fabric piece wrong side up on a flat surface and center the lid top side down on the fabric. Pull the fabric over the sides of the lid and fuse or glue in place. Carefully fold in the corners as you would to wrap a package.

3. Piece the bias strips of contrasting fabric together end-to-end using diagonal seams to create a continuous strip and press the seam allowances open.

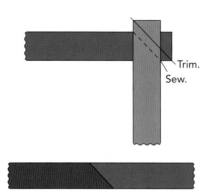

Trim.
Sew.

4. Wrap the strip around the piping cord. Stitch the tube closed using a zipper foot with the needle positioned on the left and keeping the piping cord to the left of the presser foot.

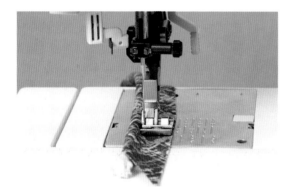

5. Apply a strip of fusible tape along the lip of the lid. Starting in the middle of the back side of the lid, place the cording on the lip of the lid and fuse in place, leaving the first 1½″ free or glue the cording in place. When you reach the starting point, overlap the ends of the cording at a 45° angle and drape the unfinished ends toward the inner part of the lid. Trim the ends to the lip of the lid and fuse the remaining cording in place.

6. Unfold the double-fold bias binding once so you can see the center and the 2 flaps. With one folded edge along the cording, glue the bias binding to the lid to finish the inside edge.

7. Use a zigzag stitch to finish all the edges of the trunk base fabric piece. Fold under one long edge 1½″ and press to create the bottom edge. Use a straight stitch to sew this hem in place for a finished edge. Fold the piece in half with right sides together and sew down the side to create a large tube. Press the seam allowance open and turn the tube right side out.

*** seam rippers 411

If you forget to sew pieces right sides together, no big deal! Just use a seam ripper to pull out the stitches and do it again.

8. Slip the fabric tube over the base of the trunk.

9. Adjust the hem of the fabric to go to the bottom edge of the trunk (the underside of the trunk will not be covered). Glue the fabric to the trunk base. Finish the top trunk edge with the bias binding as you did the edge of the trunk lid.

Sew You!

Sew decorative trim to the lid fabric before placing it on the lid. You can also use a solid fabric and one of the downloadable letters from www.makeitu.com to create a monogrammed trunk!

Sew Fun!

Using a cording foot or a welt foot will improve your accuracy in sewing down cording. See if your local sewing machine retailer carries a foot that will fit your machine.

your
space

Luggage tags

Make personalized luggage tags to identify your craft boxes, magazine holders, storage containers, and luggage. Add decorative stitching ribbons, beads, or appliqué a fun design to create your own look! The Quilter's Vinyl makes a perfect window to slip your business card into.

Supplies

* 2 pieces of fabric at least 3″ × 6″

* 1 piece of fast2fuse double-sided fusible stiff interfacing at least 3″ × 6″

* 1 piece of Quilter's Vinyl 2¾″ × 4¼″

* 15″ ribbon

* Basic Supplies

quilter's vinyl 411

Quilter's Vinyl is an amazingly versatile material. You can sew through it, write on it, and cover just about anything with it.

Use these tips for success every time:

* Always place the vinyl on top (as opposed to against the feed dogs) when you stitch it to fabric.

* Lighten your sewing machine's presser foot tension so the vinyl slides through more easily.

* Try using a walking foot or a non-stick foot.

Instructions

1. Following the manufacturer's instructions, fuse fabric to both sides of the fast2fuse.

2. Cut the fabric/fast2fuse into a rectangle 2¾″ × 5½″.

3. Trim the corners of the rectangle at 45° to make a tag shape. *Optional*: Finish the edges with a satin stitch.

4. Place Quilter's Vinyl on the squared end of the tag and sew around 3 sides using a ¼″ seam allowance, leaving the top end open to create a pocket.

5. Punch a hole in the tip of the tag using a standard hole punch. Tie a ribbon through the hole.

6. Insert your business card or address label into the Quilter's Vinyl pocket.

Fabric-Covered boxes

Do you use cardboard boxes to store your pictures? What about your recipes? Hair clips? Make your storage boxes a stylish addition to your room instead of an embarrassing eyesore!

Supplies

The yardage given is for a shoe box or a box of similar size. If you wish to cover a box of a different size, use Cutting Steps 1–3 to determine the yardage you need.

* ⅔ yard main fabric for box

* ⅝ yard contrasting fabric for box lid

* ¼˝- or ½˝-wide paper-backed fusible web tape

* Shoe box

* Water-soluble marker

* Basic supplies

Cutting

1. Measure the box width including the sides:

side + bottom + side + 1½˝ = width measurement

2. Measure the box length including the ends:

end + bottom + end + 1½˝ = length measurement

3. Repeat Steps 1 and 2 to measure the lid of the box.

4. From the main fabric, cut a rectangle the length and width of the box, as determined in Steps 1 and 2, and from the contrasting fabric cut a rectangle the length and width of the lid.

Instructions

1. Place the main fabric wrong side up and center the box on the fabric.

2. Apply the fusible tape along all 4 raw edges on the wrong side of the fabric.

3. Peel away the paper from the fusible tape on the 2 long edges of the fabric. Wrap the fabric around the box and over the edges and secure the fabric to the inside of the box. Following the manufacturer's instructions, fuse the fabric in place.

Add additional fusible tape to the folded end flap as necessary to hold it in place.

4. Peel away the paper from the fusible tape on the short edges of the fabric. Fold the fabric around the box as if you were wrapping a present and fuse the fabric in place.

5. Repeat Steps 1–4 with the contrasting fabric to cover the lid.

Sew You!

Create your own fabric by scanning pictures of family or friends and printing them on printable fabric sheets. Sew the pieces of fabric sheets together to make a piece big enough to cover your box.

Sew Fun!

To make a lightweight fabric heavier, use a fusible batting or lightweight interfacing. This technique will make cottons and silks crisper and heavier, similar to the weight of linen or denim.

Memo board

Many of us carry our dreams around in our hearts and heads—here's an opportunity to put them somewhere where you can reflect on them from time to time.

Supplies

* 20″ × 30″ × 3/16″ foamcore board
* 1/2 yard background fabric
* 3/4 yard outer-border fabric
* 1/2 yard piping fabric
* 3 yards 1/4″ cording for piping
* 3/4 yard low-loft batting
* 7/8 yard nonwoven fleece interfacing
* 6 1/2 yards flat braid
* Temporary fabric adhesive spray
* Small beads
* Assorted charms or large beads (optional)
* Metal glue for charms (optional)
* Stapler
* Basic supplies

Cutting

1. FROM THE BACKGROUND FABRIC: Cut 1 rectangle 25 1/2″ × 15 1/2″.

2. FROM THE OUTER-BORDER FABRIC: Cut 3 strips 6″ by the width of the fabric. Subcut 1 strip into 2 rectangles 6″ × 15 1/2″ and the remaining strips into 2 rectangles 6″ × 36 1/2″.

3. FROM THE PIPING FABRIC: Cut enough 1 1/2″-wide bias strips to total at least 120″ long.

4. FROM THE NONWOVEN FLEECE INTERFACING: Cut 1 rectangle 26″ × 36″.

5. FROM THE BATTING: Cut 1 rectangle 24″ × 34″.

Instructions

Sew all pieces right sides together, using a 1/4″ seam allowance.

1. Place the foamcore board on a flat surface and apply temporary fabric adhesive spray. Center the batting on the foamcore and press to adhere.

2. Spray the batting with adhesive and position the fleece on top, smoothing the surface to remove any lumps. Set aside.

3. Place the background fabric on a flat surface and pencil a grid of diagonal lines 4″ apart. Position the braid along all the diagonal lines, first in one direction and then in the opposite direction, cutting the pieces of braid as you go along. Adjust the braid as necessary and pin in place. Stitch around the background fabric about ⅛″ away from the raw edge to secure the ends of the braid. Leave the pins in position to hold the rest of braid in place.

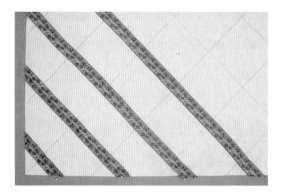

4. Stitch the 1½″-wide bias strips together end-to-end (see Step 3, page 64). Press the seam allowances open.

5. Place the cording in the center of the bias strip then fold it in half over the cording. Use a zipper foot with the needle to the left and a basting stitch to sew the cording inside the folded strip. Trim the seam allowance on the piping to ¼″.

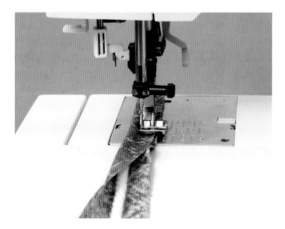

6. Align the raw edges of the piping with the raw edges of the background fabric. Start at the middle of the bottom edge of the background fabric and leave 1½″ of the cording free. Pin and baste the piping in place. Clip the seam allowance of the piping at the corners. When you reach the starting point, overlap the ends of the cording at a 45° angle and drape the unfinished ends toward the edge of the background fabric. Trim the ends and baste in place.

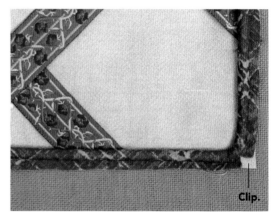

Clip.

7. Pin the side borders in place, aligning all the raw edges. Use a zipper foot to stitch on top of the line of basting stitches. Press the seam allowances toward the borders. Repeat with the top and bottom borders, stitching these borders to the edges of the side borders. Press the seam allowances toward the borders.

8. Turn the edges of the completed top under ½″ on all sides and press. Center the top on the foamcore, placing a few pins to secure it.

9. Turn the foamcore over and staple the folded edge of the top to the back side of the foamcore in the center of all 4 sides, pulling the fabric taut. Continue to staple around the pressed edges, keeping a consistent tension on the main fabric. Turn the foamcore right side up.

10. At each braid intersection, hand sew a small bead to hold the trim in place. For an extra decorative touch, add charms or large beads.

Sew You!

Glue inspirational words to your board or add mementos from your favorite trips or concerts. Photos of friends, family, and inspirational places can be tucked underneath the braid to hold them in place.

Check out Fast, Fun & Easy® Home Accents by Pam Archer from C&T Publishing for more on making neat things for around the house.

Whether you are wishing someone Happy Birthday or sending an invitation, these fabric cards stand out as uniquely you. Create a card that sets your message apart from others'.

Fabric cards

Supplies

* 2 pieces of fabric, each somewhat larger than the card size

* Small scraps of fabric for embellishments

* Paper-backed fusible web or fast2fuse double-sided fusible stiff interfacing

* Printer paper

* Trim, beads, buttons, crystals, ribbon, glitter, etc.

* Non-stick pressing sheet (optional)

* Basic supplies

Fusible Web Instructions

1. Decide what size and shape card you want and cut 2 pieces of fabric at least ¾″ larger than these dimensions. For a folding card, remember to make the fabric pieces large enough to be folded in half.

2. Cut 2 pieces of fusible web, each about ¼″ smaller than the fabric pieces.

3. Center the fusible web on the wrong side of each fabric piece and, following the manufacturer's instructions, fuse in place. Remove the paper backing as one piece and save it for later.

*paper backing 411

The paper backing from fusible web makes a great protective sheet for your ironing board. The paper will keep any excess fusible web from sticking to your ironing board or iron. A non-stick pressing sheet serves the same purpose and is a good investment if you do a lot of fusing.

4. Layer one of the fabric pieces (fusible side up), a sheet of printer paper, and the remaining fabric piece (fusible side down). Following the manufacturer's instructions, fuse these layers together. The printer paper will give the card some stiffness.

5. Use a rotary cutter to cut the fabric sandwich to the desired dimensions. For a folding card, fold the piece in half and press well to crease.

6. Fuse web to scraps of various fabrics and cut out shapes like balloons, hearts, candles, or whatever you want on the card. Remove the paper backing, arrange the shapes on the front of the card, and fuse them in place.

7. Stitch around the edges or glue pieces of trim over the outer edges of the card to give it a finished look. Use a fine-tip marker to write a message on the card or use fabric paints and glitter to give the card some sparkle.

fast2fuse Instructions

1. Decide what size and shape card you want and cut pieces of fast2fuse to these dimensions. For a flat, single-panel card, cut a single piece of fast2fuse. For a folding card, cut 2 pieces of fast2fuse of equal size.

✱✱ ✱ fast2fuse 411

Fast2fuse, which combines fusible web with stiff interfacing, gives cards some thickness and dimensionality.

2. For a flat card, cut 2 pieces of fabric to the same size as the fast2fuse piece.

3. For a folding card, cut 2 pieces of fabric the same width as the fast2fuse pieces and ¼″ longer than their combined lengths to accomodate the fold in the card.

4. Place the fast2fuse pieces on the wrong side of 1 fabric piece. For the folding card, leave ¼″ of space between the fast2fuse panels for the fold in the card. Layer the second fabric piece on top and, following the manufacturer's instructions, fuse everything together.

5. Zigzag stitch or glue pieces of trim over the outer edges of the card to give it a finished look. Glue buttons or beads to the front to make it uniquely you! Use a fine-tip marker to write a message on the card or use fabric paints and glitter to give the card special personality.

✱ ✱
✱ Check out Spectacular Cards by Sue Astroth from C&T Publishing for more on making all kinds of fun cards.

Sew You!

Use the same techniques to make your own scrapbook. Preserve memories of your favorite people, experiences, or places using fabric, embellishments, and the endless possibilities of a blank board book from C&T Publishing. These books come in fun shapes like purses, houses, tags, accordions, and more!

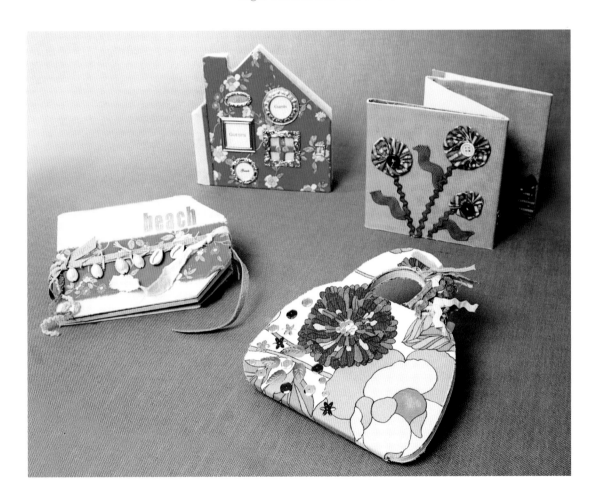

Fabric Vase

Showcase dried flowers with this eye-catching vase to give bookshelves and tabletops a unique look. Use your favorite fabrics to match your décor and put a finishing touch on a room.

Supplies

* Fat quarter for inside of vase

* Coordinating fat quarter for outside of vase

* ¼ yard fast2fuse double-sided fusible stiff interfacing

* Thread to coordinate with the fabrics

* Cardboard or template plastic

* Basic supplies

fat quarter 411

Many quilt shops sell fat quarters. Instead of being a 9″ strip from selvage to selvage like a normal ¼ yard, fat quarters are ½ of a ½-yard cut, creating a rectangular 18″ × 22″ shape.

Cutting

1. Trace the vase side and base patterns on page 85 onto template plastic or cardboard and cut out the templates.

2. From the fast2fuse, cut 2 rectangles 8″ × 9″ and 1 rectangle 3″ × 4½″.

3. From the inside fabric, cut 2 rectangles 8″ × 9″ and 1 rectangle 3″ × 4½″. Repeat for the outside fabric.

Instructions

1. Following the manufacturer's instructions, fuse one inside fabric piece to one side of each fast2fuse rectangle. Fuse the outside fabric pieces to the other sides of the fast2fuse rectangles.

2. On the inside fabric, use the templates to trace 2 vase sides and 1 base on the fabric sandwich pieces, and cut out the shapes.

3. Select a wide zigzag stitch (width 3.5, length 0.2 or 0.3) and satin stitch around the edges of each piece with coordinating thread.

4. Select a narrow zigzag stitch (width 1.5, length 1.5) to sew the sides to the base. Align the corner edge of the elliptical base with the bottom edge of a vase side. Keep the base on top while sewing and match up the edges as you go. The right stitch of the zigzag stitch should go out over the edge of the pieces. You want to just catch the edge of the satin stitching on both pieces.

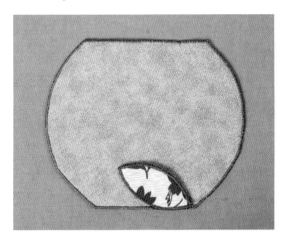

5. Start by sewing several stitches in place or by back tacking. Pull the base to meet the edge of the side as you sew. Back tack at the end of the seam. The side will curl up and begin to shape itself as it passes under the presser foot. If the ends don't quite match, it's okay; when you sew the sides together, you can cover the mismatch.

6. Sew the other side to the base in the same way, beginning at the end of the base opposite the end you started with in Step 5. You will need to bend or fold the stiff interfacing to fit the vase under the presser foot.

7. Fold the 2 halves of the vase together and pin the top edge on one side.

8. Begin sewing down the side from the top. You will need to fold the base in half to do this. Remember to back tack at the beginning and end of the seam. Sew the second side in the same way.

9. Use a steam iron to press the base and hold it on something flat until it cools and holds the shape you want.

10. Use a steam iron to press the sides as necessary. Just hold the vase in the shape you want or place something round in it while it cools. It will get quite hot, so save your fingers and use a glass, a jar, or a ball of string to help steam the lip to a rounded shape.

* *
* Check out *Fast, Fun & Easy® Fabric Vases* by *Linda Johansen* from *C&T Publishing* for more on making all kinds of fabric vases.

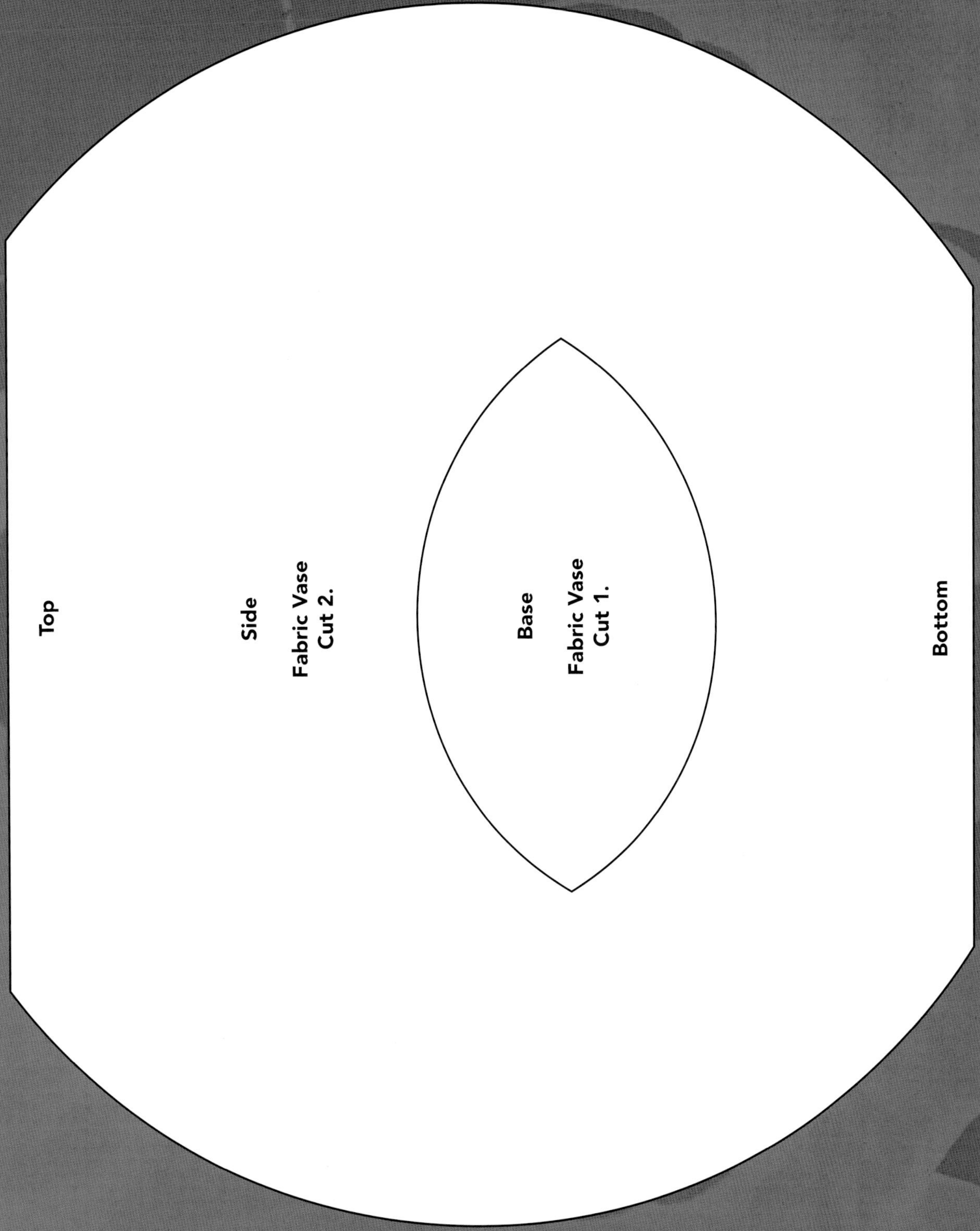

Top

Side

**Fabric Vase
Cut 2.**

Base

**Fabric Vase
Cut 1.**

Bottom

Sources

Check out these places to find what you need to get started!

Cactus Punch
machine embroidery collections
www.cactuspunch.com
1-800-933-8081

C&T Publishing
*fast2fuse double-sided fusible stiff
interfacing, Quilters Vinyl, projects, and
project templates*
www.ctpub.com
1-800-284-1114

Husqvarna Viking Sewing Machines
*sewing machines, feet, and related
accessories*
www.husqvarnaviking.com
1-800-446-2333

Inspira Notions
stabilizers and assorted notions
1-800-446-2333

Kandi Corp
hot-fix decorative applicator and crystals
www.kandicorp.com
1-800-985-2634

Pfaff Sewing Machines
*sewing machines, feet, and related
accessories*
www.pfaffusa.com
1-800-446-2333

RJR Fabrics
fabrics
www.rjrfabrics.com
1-800-422-5426

Sulky of America
KK 2000 temporary spray adhesive
www.sulky.com
1-800-874-4115

Tsukineko
inks
www.tsukineko.com
1-425-883-7733

The Warm Company
Steam-A-Seam fusible web and batting
www.warmcompany.com

YLI Threads
decorative threads and cording
www.ylicorp.com
1-800-296-8139

acknowledgments

To Amy Marson and C&T Publishing—Thank you for your belief in this project and for making this book possible, for putting a vision into pictures and words that the whole world can share with us.

Rick Cohen and RJR Fabrics—Thank you for such beautiful pieces of art to work with. Your drive and dedication to this project are evident.

To Tina Battock and CK Media—Thank you for your support of MIY. Your willingness to help us spread the word is crucial, and your execution in this task is amazing.

To Nancy Jewell and Sue Hausmann at VSM Sewing Inc.—Thank you for your passion and creativity and for helping us keep sewing alive and spread it to new people in any way we can.

dedication

To my sisters, my family, and my friends for their support, inspiration, and drive. To my Jeff, without whom none of this would have been possible. Thank you for all your love and support and your belief in who I am.

project credits

Curtains, valance, sink skirt, embellished towels, bed canopy, screen panels, framed fabrics, fabric wallpaper border, fabric-covered frames, covered storage trunk, and fabric-covered boxes made by Shannon Mullen. Pillows and quilt made by Liz Aneloski. Memo board made by Cyndy Rymer. Fabric vases made by Lynn Koolish. Fabric cards made by Stacy Chamness, Kiera Lofgreen, and Kesel Wilson. Luggage tags made by Gailen Runge. Special thanks to Carolyn Aune for her technical expertise.

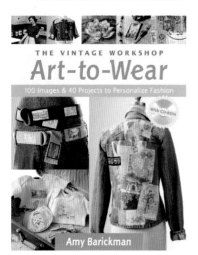
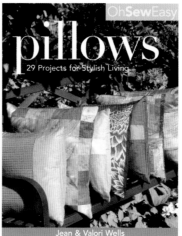